THE
Sixty Second
FAMILY

The Sixty Minute Marriage
The Sixty Minute Mother
The Sixty Second Family
The Sixty Second Father
The Sixty Second Marriage
The Wisdom House
What Every Kid Wished Their Parents Knew ... and Vice Versa
What They Didn't Teach Me in Sunday School

And by Dianne Parsons

The Sixty Second Mother

THE
Sixty Second
FAMILY

ROB PARSONS

To the memory of Rosa Algieri –
a wonderful mother, grandmother and great-grandmother.

Acknowledgements

Special thanks to Alice Instone-Brewer and Sheron Rice for their fantastic help with this little collection of quotes. And many thanks also to designer Allison Hodgkiss, and Kim Davies, June Way and the team at Care for the Family.

There are so many words we could use in relation to families: warmth, fun, arguments, acts of kindness, hard work, frustration, joy, pain, worry, intimacy ... And above all, of course, there's that little word love. In this book of quotations I have tried to capture some of these different aspects of family life. They are the thoughts of all sorts of people – both the famous and ordinary folk like you and me. Some will make you think, some may cause a tear, and some will make you laugh out loud. I do hope you enjoy it.

Rob Parsons, OBE

We need our family. It's the place where we discover who we are – our gifts and ambitions, our hopes and fears. It's the people who help us prepare to face a whole world, to learn what works and what doesn't.

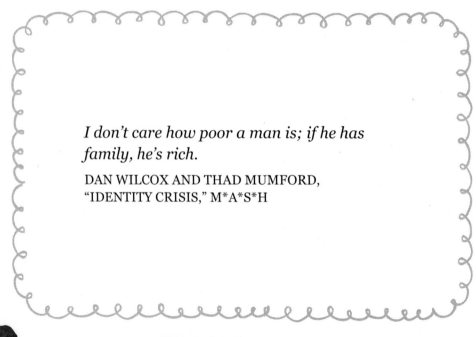

I don't care how poor a man is; if he has family, he's rich.

DAN WILCOX AND THAD MUMFORD,
"IDENTITY CRISIS," M*A*S*H

THE SIXTY SECOND FAMILY

Family is the most important thing in the world.
PRINCESS DIANA

All the laws and legislation in the world will never heal this world like the loving hearts and arms of mothers and fathers. If every child could drift to sleep feeling wrapped in the love of their family – and God's love – this world would be a far more gentle and better place.

MITT ROMNEY

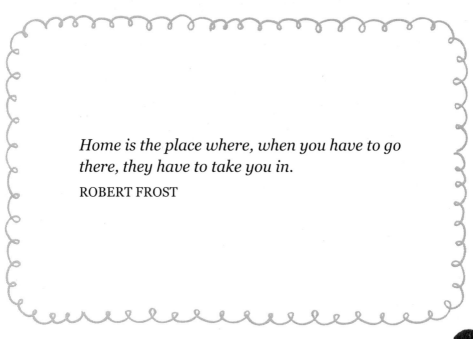

Home is the place where, when you have to go there, they have to take you in.

ROBERT FROST

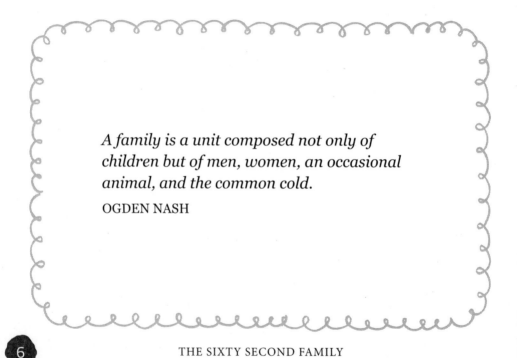

A family is a unit composed not only of children but of men, women, an occasional animal, and the common cold.

OGDEN NASH

I am convinced that material things can contribute a lot to making one's life pleasant, but, basically, if you do not have very good friends and relatives who matter to you, life will be really empty and sad and material things cease to be important."

DAVID ROCKEFELLER

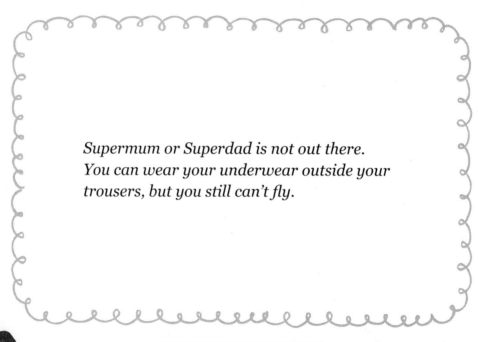

Supermum or Superdad is not out there.
You can wear your underwear outside your
trousers, but you still can't fly.

THE SIXTY SECOND FAMILY

When I get a headache I take two asprin and keep away from the children – just like it says on the bottle.

AUTHOR UNKNOWN

People who say they sleep like a baby usually don't have one.

AUTHOR UNKNOWN

The great gift of family life is to be intimately acquainted with people you might never even introduce yourself to, had life not done it for you.

KENDALL HAILEY

Like all the best families, we have our share of eccentricities, of impetuous and wayward youngsters and of family disagreements.

ELIZABETH II

THE SIXTY SECOND FAMILY

Our most basic instinct is not for survival but for family. Most of us would give our own life for the survival of a family member, yet we lead our daily life too often as if we take our family for granted."

PAUL PEARSHALL

No matter what you've done for yourself or for humanity, if you can't look back on having given love and attention to your own family, what have you really accomplished?

LEE IACOCCA

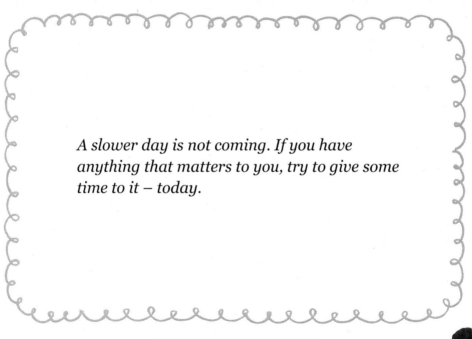

A slower day is not coming. If you have anything that matters to you, try to give some time to it – today.

When my children were small, the years ahead seemed like the start of the long summer holiday when we were kids – practically eternal. But then somebody suggested imagining that an egg-timer contained not sand but days. It's sobering. When your child is born, the timer has

THE SIXTY SECOND FAMILY

6,570 days in it – the number of days until they reach eighteen. If your child is ten, 3,650 days have already gone – you have 2,920 left. No amount of money, power or prestige can increase that number by a single day.

Just at the moment when we finally have time for our children, they've learned to say, "Great idea, Dad. But would you mind if we did it later?"

THE SIXTY SECOND FAMILY

We are so busy giving our kids what we didn't have that we don't have time to give them what we did have.

Always kiss your children goodnight – even if they're already asleep.

H. JACKSON BROWN, JR.

THE SIXTY SECOND FAMILY

The simple secret of families that have time for each other is that they've made it a priority – they actually plan for it.

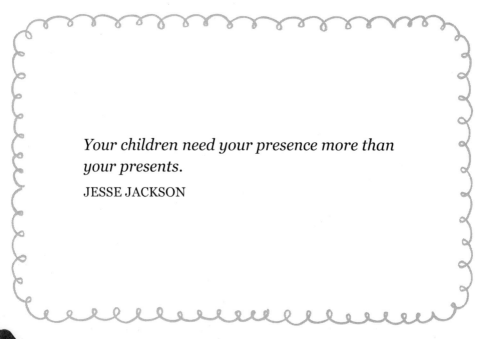

Your children need your presence more than your presents.

JESSE JACKSON

A father is someone who carries pictures in his wallet where his money used to be.

AUTHOR UNKNOWN

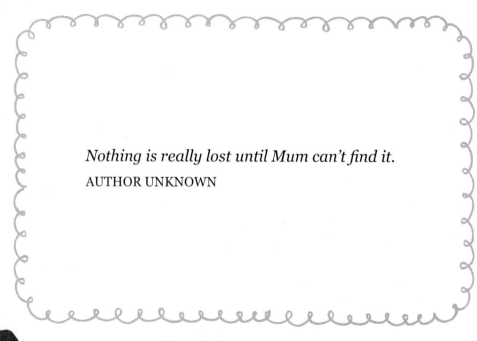

Nothing is really lost until Mum can't find it.

AUTHOR UNKNOWN

THE SIXTY SECOND FAMILY

A small girl approached her father as he was busily entering appointments into his planner. She asked, "Dad, what are you doing?" He didn't look up from his task, just mumbled, "I'm putting in times when I can see some really important people." She said, "Dad, am I in that book?"

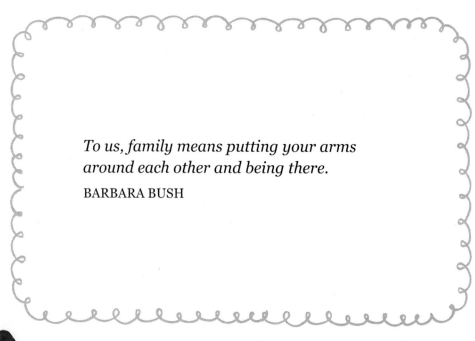

To us, family means putting your arms around each other and being there.

BARBARA BUSH

THE SIXTY SECOND FAMILY

Communication with our family is vital. This doesn't have to be complicated. It could be just chatting as we do ordinary things together – clearing out the garage, helping with homework or cleaning out the rabbit hutch.

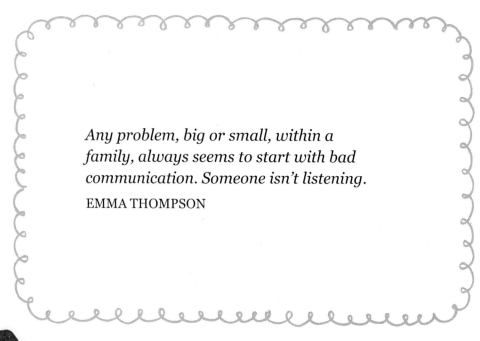

Any problem, big or small, within a family, always seems to start with bad communication. Someone isn't listening.

EMMA THOMPSON

THE SIXTY SECOND FAMILY

My father used to play with my brother and me in the yard. Mother would come out and say, "You're tearing up the grass."

"We're not raising grass," Dad would reply. "We're raising boys."

HARMON KILLEBREW

Smile at each other. Smile at your wife, smile at your husband, smile at your children, smile at each other – it doesn't matter who it is – and that will help you to grow up in greater love for each other.

MOTHER TERESA

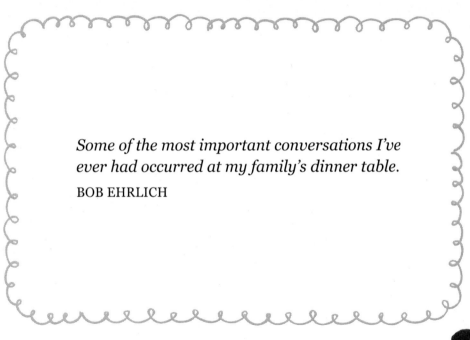

Some of the most important conversations I've ever had occurred at my family's dinner table.

BOB EHRLICH

THE SIXTY SECOND FAMILY

31

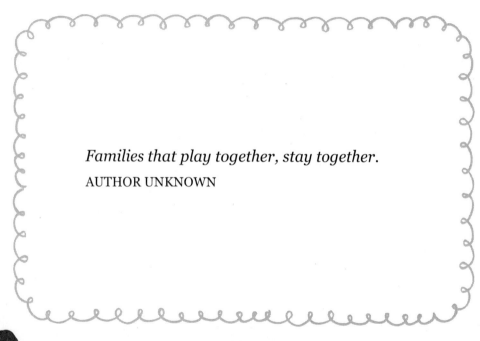

Families that play together, stay together.
AUTHOR UNKNOWN

THE SIXTY SECOND FAMILY

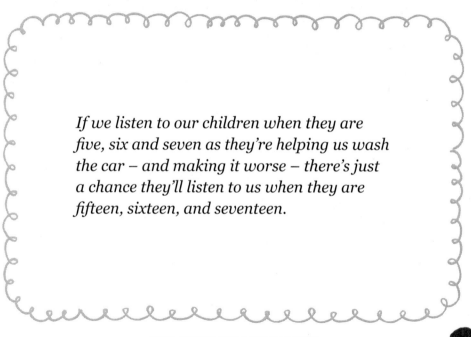

If we listen to our children when they are five, six and seven as they're helping us wash the car – and making it worse – there's just a chance they'll listen to us when they are fifteen, sixteen, and seventeen.

THE SIXTY SECOND FAMILY

33

Ask your kids for their opinions on things – trivial and serious; it's part of their growing-up process.

THE SIXTY SECOND FAMILY

It takes careful thought and determination but it's possible to organise meaningful mealtimes – without television, without just gulping things down on the run. Family meals are important even if you only have one family meal each week.

STEPHEN R. COVEY

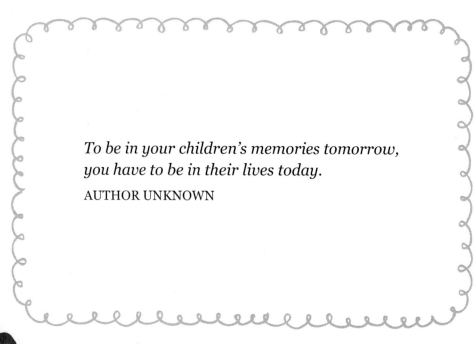

To be in your children's memories tomorrow, you have to be in their lives today.

AUTHOR UNKNOWN

THE SIXTY SECOND FAMILY

Enforcing the rules is not just a matter of discipline; it is a matter of security ... There is no faster way to breed insecurity in a child than for them to believe there are no boundaries – and that even if there are, nobody cares if they are crossed.

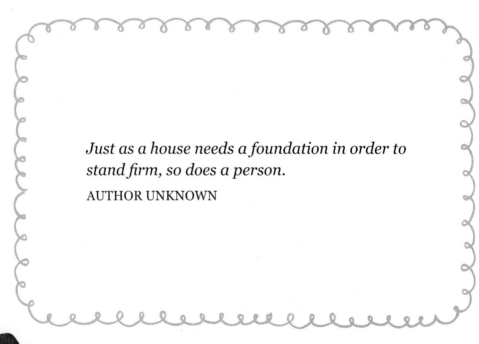

Just as a house needs a foundation in order to stand firm, so does a person.

AUTHOR UNKNOWN

THE SIXTY SECOND FAMILY

Our children will test the boundaries – push against them every now and then to test they are still there. They will actually feel more secure knowing they are in place.

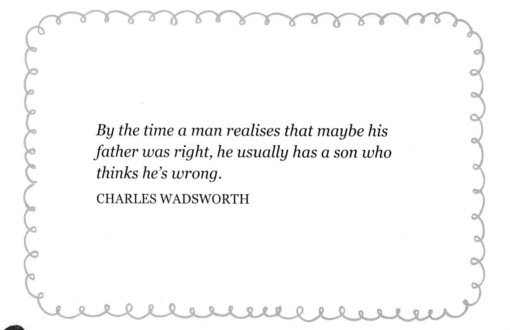

By the time a man realises that maybe his father was right, he usually has a son who thinks he's wrong.

CHARLES WADSWORTH

THE SIXTY SECOND FAMILY

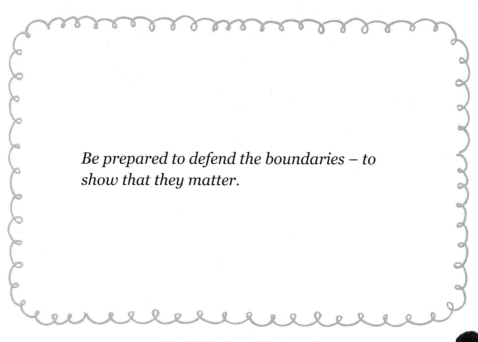

Be prepared to defend the boundaries – to show that they matter.

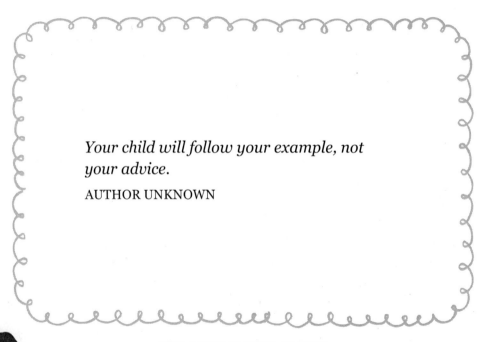

Your child will follow your example, not your advice.

AUTHOR UNKNOWN

When it comes to their own children, there are no 'experts' – just people trying to get their own families through as best they can.

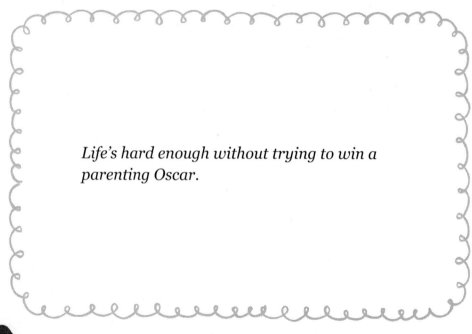

Life's hard enough without trying to win a parenting Oscar.

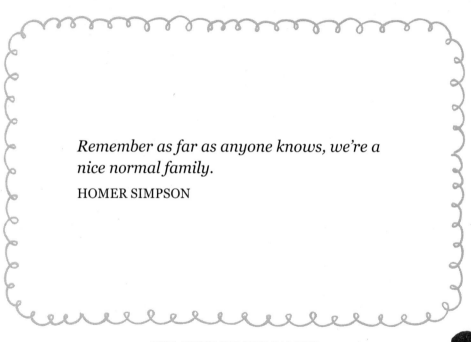

Remember as far as anyone knows, we're a nice normal family.

HOMER SIMPSON

THE SIXTY SECOND FAMILY

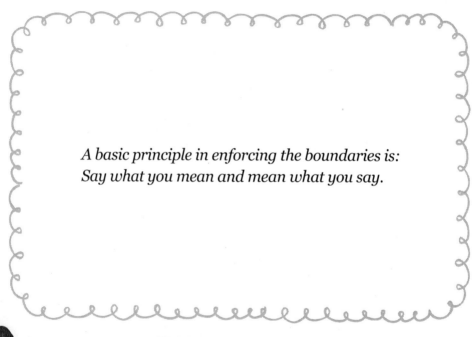

*A basic principle in enforcing the boundaries is:
Say what you mean and mean what you say.*

THE SIXTY SECOND FAMILY

The values we pass on to our children are not only taught – but caught. The scary thing is not that our children aren't listening to us – but that they are.

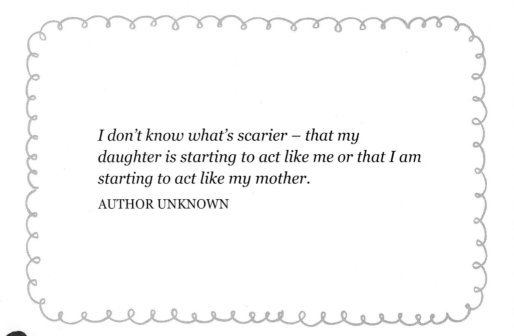

I don't know what's scarier – that my daughter is starting to act like me or that I am starting to act like my mother.

AUTHOR UNKNOWN

THE SIXTY SECOND FAMILY

Rules without relationship lead to rebellion.

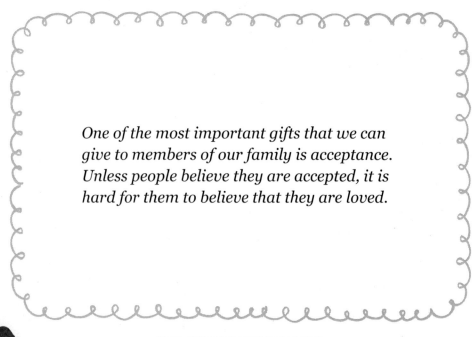

One of the most important gifts that we can give to members of our family is acceptance. Unless people believe they are accepted, it is hard for them to believe that they are loved.

THE SIXTY SECOND FAMILY

Sometimes we have to love our kids when we don't 'like' them very much.

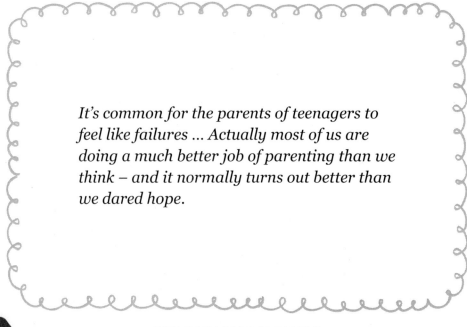

It's common for the parents of teenagers to feel like failures ... Actually most of us are doing a much better job of parenting than we think – and it normally turns out better than we dared hope.

THE SIXTY SECOND FAMILY

That's what people do who love you. They put their arms around you and love you when you're not so lovable.

DEB CALETTI

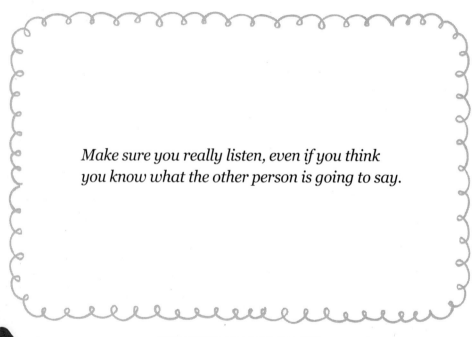

Make sure you really listen, even if you think you know what the other person is going to say.

THE SIXTY SECOND FAMILY

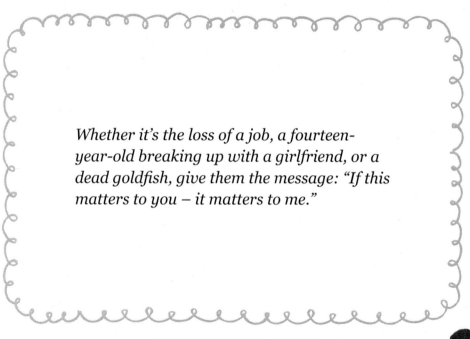

Whether it's the loss of a job, a fourteen-year-old breaking up with a girlfriend, or a dead goldfish, give them the message: "If this matters to you – it matters to me."

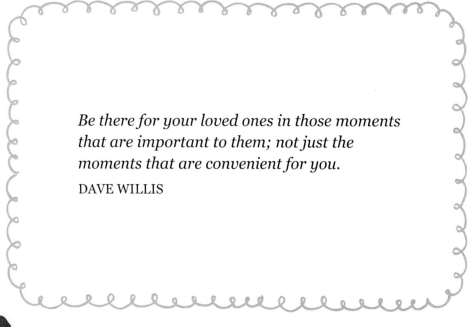

Be there for your loved ones in those moments that are important to them; not just the moments that are convenient for you.

DAVE WILLIS

THE SIXTY SECOND FAMILY

The love of the family, the love of the person can heal. It heals the scars left by a larger society. A massive, powerful society.

MAYA ANGELOU

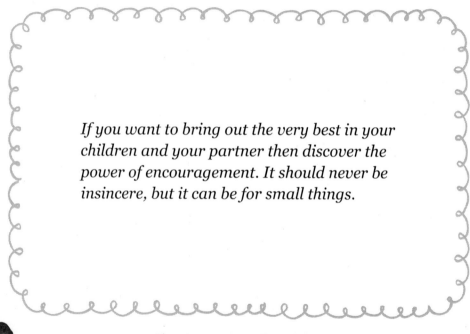

If you want to bring out the very best in your children and your partner then discover the power of encouragement. It should never be insincere, but it can be for small things.

58

Don't strive for perfection. Remember the letter the head teacher used to send home with the kids on the first day of school:

Dear Parent

If you promise not to believe all that your child tells you goes on at school,

I promise not to believe all that they tell me goes on at home.

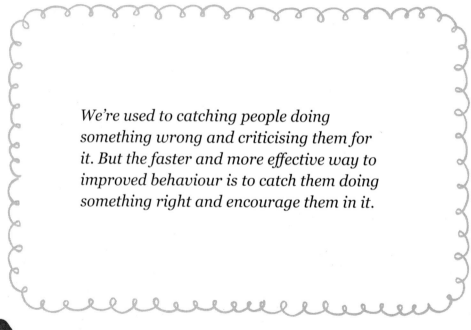

We're used to catching people doing something wrong and criticising them for it. But the faster and more effective way to improved behaviour is to catch them doing something right and encourage them in it.

THE SIXTY SECOND FAMILY

Affirmation can become an attitude.

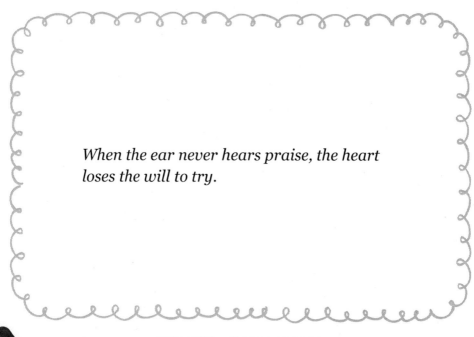

When the ear never hears praise, the heart loses the will to try.

THE SIXTY SECOND FAMILY

When your mother asks, "Do you want a piece of advice?" it's a mere formality. It doesn't matter if you answer yes or no. You're going to get it anyway.

ERMA BOMBECK

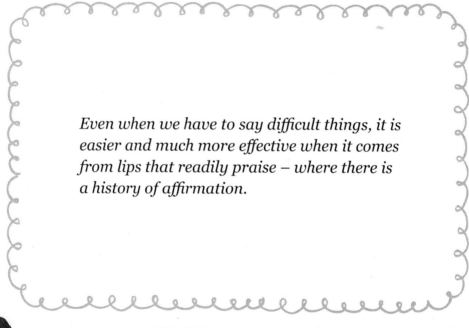

Even when we have to say difficult things, it is easier and much more effective when it comes from lips that readily praise – where there is a history of affirmation.

THE SIXTY SECOND FAMILY

If you ever want to call a family meeting, just turn off the wi-fi and wait in the family room in which it's located.

AUTHOR UNKNOWN

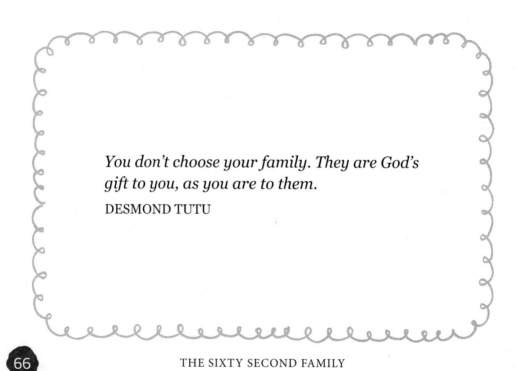

You don't choose your family. They are God's gift to you, as you are to them.

DESMOND TUTU

THE SIXTY SECOND FAMILY

More important than how much conflict we have in our family is how we resolve it. Strong families don't avoid conflict; they develop effective strategies to deal with it.

The greatest thing in family life is to take a hint when a hint is intended – and not to take a hint when a hint is not intended.

ROBERT FROST

Don't attack somebody's person. Your partner may be able to handle a row about her missing your daughter's dental appointment, but expect long-term trouble if you start using phrases like, "You're such a lousy wife and mother."

Give the other person a chance to speak without interrupting – and listen.

THE SIXTY SECOND FAMILY

The silliest line in any film ever is found in the blockbuster Love Story: *"Love means never having to say you're sorry." In fact the opposite is true: "Love means always having to say you're sorry."*

Don't dig up dirt from the past. "I'll never forget when you ..." Every marriage has two or three old bazookas that the couple bring out in time of conflict. Lay them down (if only to find new ones!)

If you feel you're about to explode, try to hold your tongue for a moment and ask yourself three questions:

Is this really important to me?

When I look at the facts, is my anger justified?

How can I contribute to the solution?

A healthy family requires frequent use of three phrases: "May I ... ?", "Thank you", and "I'm sorry." And never, ever end the day without making peace.

POPE FRANCIS

THE SIXTY SECOND FAMILY

"I think all kids should have the right to live in a happy place where they feel safe and loved. I haven't felt like that in some time, but I know my parents don't mean it. It's just that they argue and take it out on me."

14-YEAR-OLD BOY

What can you do to promote world peace? Go home and love your family.

MOTHER THERESA

THE SIXTY SECOND FAMILY

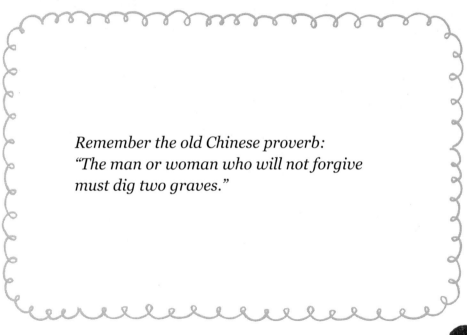

Remember the old Chinese proverb:
"The man or woman who will not forgive
must dig two graves."

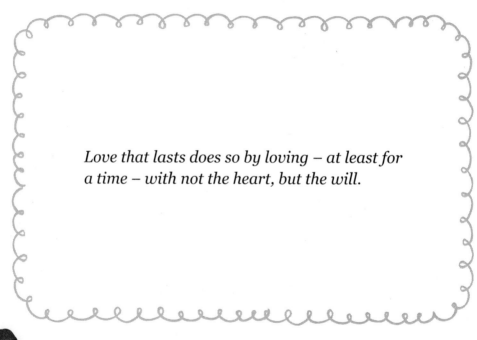

Love that lasts does so by loving – at least for a time – with not the heart, but the will.

THE SIXTY SECOND FAMILY

*The antidote to 'a creeping separateness' –
simply drifting apart – is not usually found in
expensive holidays, or what some have called
quality time, but in quite a lot of ordinary time.*

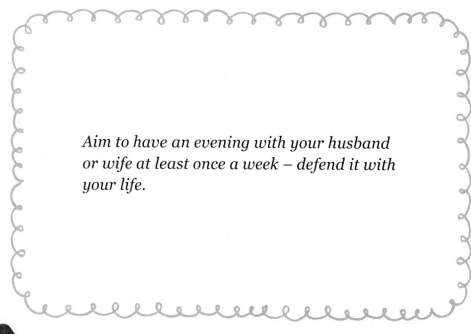

Aim to have an evening with your husband or wife at least once a week – defend it with your life.

THE SIXTY SECOND FAMILY

Every relationship is a compromise.

THE SIXTY SECOND FAMILY

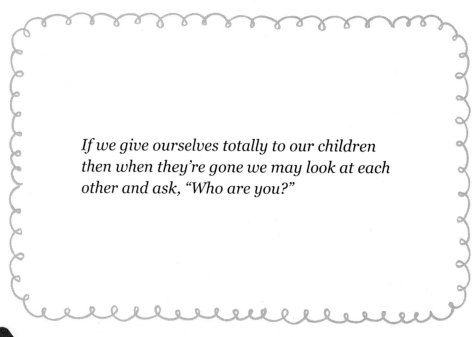

If we give ourselves totally to our children then when they're gone we may look at each other and ask, "Who are you?"

THE SIXTY SECOND FAMILY

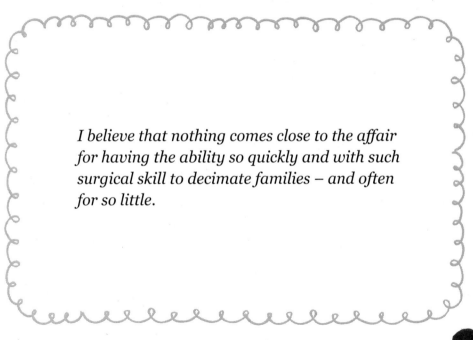

I believe that nothing comes close to the affair for having the ability so quickly and with such surgical skill to decimate families – and often for so little.

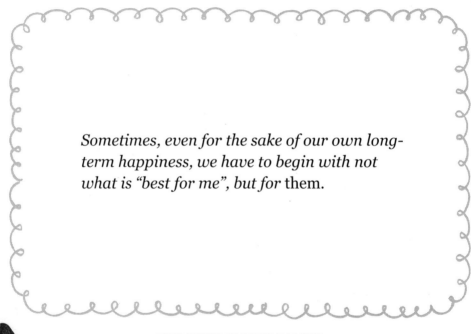

Sometimes, even for the sake of our own long-term happiness, we have to begin with not what is "best for me", but for them.

THE SIXTY SECOND FAMILY

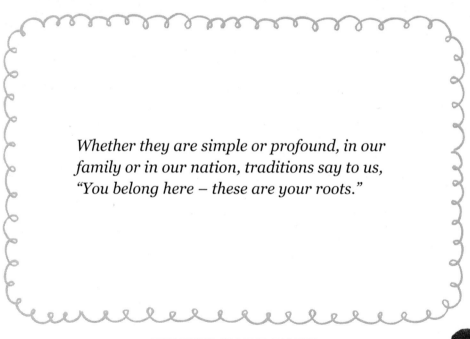

Whether they are simple or profound, in our family or in our nation, traditions say to us, "You belong here – these are your roots."

THE SIXTY SECOND FAMILY

Each day of our lives we make deposits in the memory banks of our children.

CHARLES R. SWINDOLL

THE SIXTY SECOND FAMILY

Don't relegate the humble table to some past "golden age of the family" – there never was such a time. The fact is that whether it's eating together, working together, or playing together, the table can be a focal point in our family life.

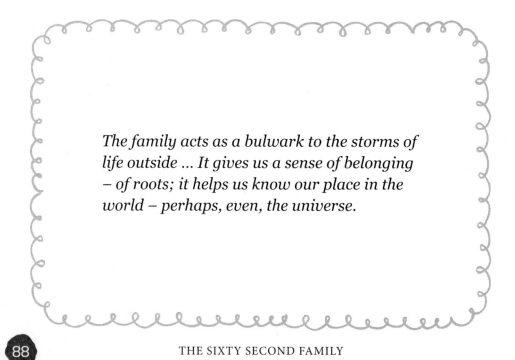

The family acts as a bulwark to the storms of life outside ... It gives us a sense of belonging – of roots; it helps us know our place in the world – perhaps, even, the universe.

THE SIXTY SECOND FAMILY

Traditions are powerful. If you don't believe me then talk to any adult you know who had a happy family life. Ask them to tell you what made it special and pretty soon they'll say, "We always ..."

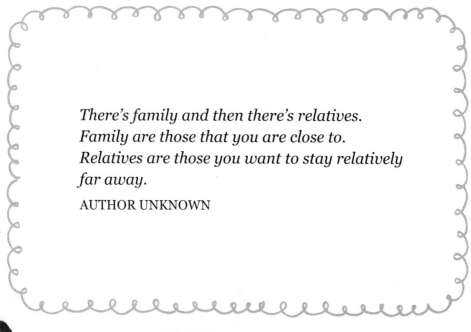

There's family and then there's relatives.
Family are those that you are close to.
Relatives are those you want to stay relatively
far away.

AUTHOR UNKNOWN

THE SIXTY SECOND FAMILY

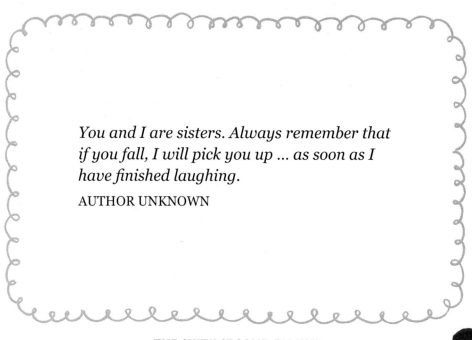

You and I are sisters. Always remember that if you fall, I will pick you up ... as soon as I have finished laughing.

AUTHOR UNKNOWN

The extended family is important for our children. It's good for them to have an understanding of not just the 'roots' of our family, but the 'branches'.

THE SIXTY SECOND FAMILY

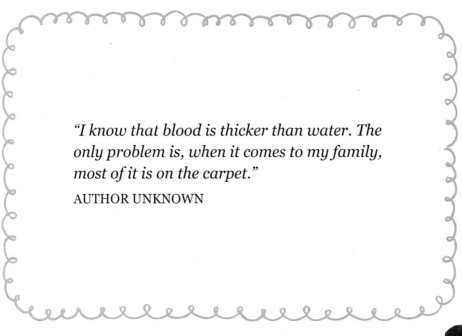

"I know that blood is thicker than water. The only problem is, when it comes to my family, most of it is on the carpet."

AUTHOR UNKNOWN

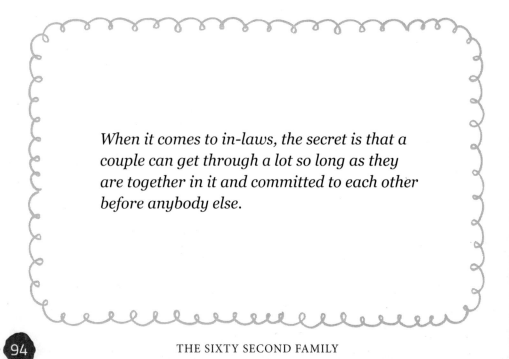

When it comes to in-laws, the secret is that a couple can get through a lot so long as they are together in it and committed to each other before anybody else.

THE SIXTY SECOND FAMILY

"People have no idea of the guilt sometimes involved in trying to do your best for somebody you love with all your heart. I know that I simply can't provide the 24-hour care my mum needs, yet the guilt almost chokes me."

AUTHOR UNKNOWN

Special people in our life sometimes can become our family, it doesn't mean they have to be blood related, it means appreciating those who care and love you.

B. B. BUTLER

THE SIXTY SECOND FAMILY

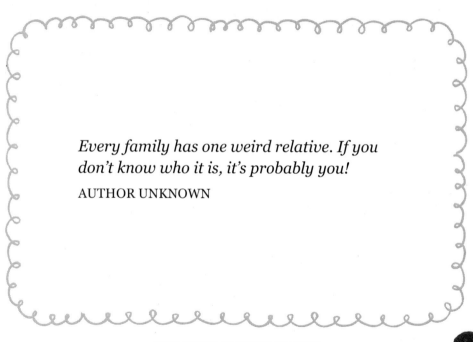

Every family has one weird relative. If you don't know who it is, it's probably you!

AUTHOR UNKNOWN

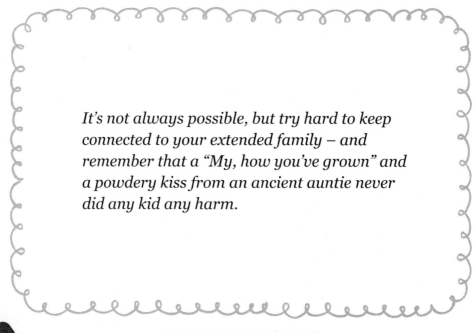

It's not always possible, but try hard to keep connected to your extended family – and remember that a "My, how you've grown" and a powdery kiss from an ancient auntie never did any kid any harm.

THE SIXTY SECOND FAMILY

Encourage your parents to tell stories from 'the old days'. Even though we may be bored of them, to our kids they are often magical.

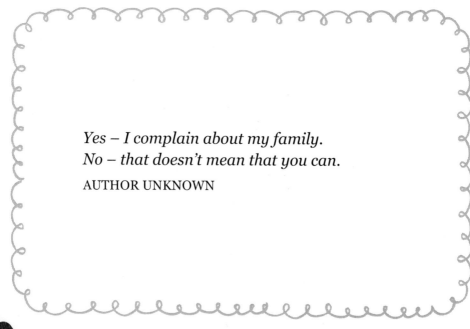

Yes – I complain about my family.
No – that doesn't mean that you can.

AUTHOR UNKNOWN

THE SIXTY SECOND FAMILY

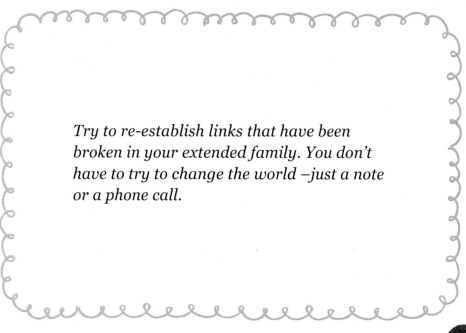

Try to re-establish links that have been broken in your extended family. You don't have to try to change the world –just a note or a phone call.

THE SIXTY SECOND FAMILY

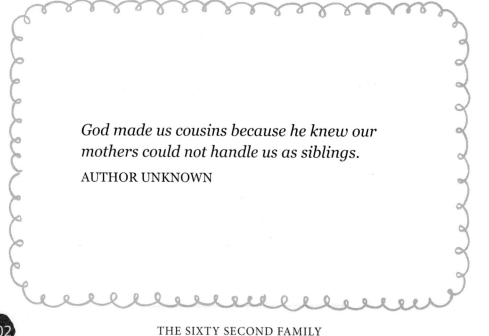

God made us cousins because he knew our mothers could not handle us as siblings.

AUTHOR UNKNOWN

THE SIXTY SECOND FAMILY

Older siblings: the only people who will pick on you for their own entertainment and beat up anyone else who tries.

AUTHOR UNKNOWN

Somebody one said: "Good judgement is based on experience and experience is based on bad judgement." The problem when we take so much control of our children's lives that we make everything come right for them is that we rob them of the learning process that comes with a little pain.

THE SIXTY SECOND FAMILY

Dearest child,

I've worried for you since before you were born. I'll continue to worry for you until my last breath. Deal with it!

Love Mum.

AUTHOR UNKNOWN

With our older children we have to realise that they'll make their own choices – and sometimes those may be bad ones.

THE SIXTY SECOND FAMILY

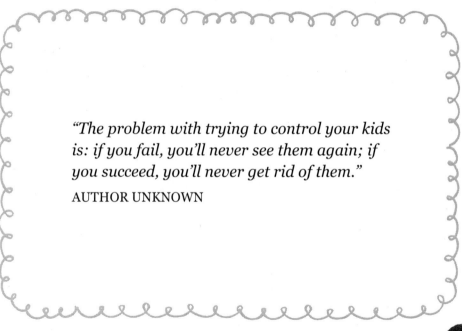

"The problem with trying to control your kids is: if you fail, you'll never see them again; if you succeed, you'll never get rid of them."

AUTHOR UNKNOWN

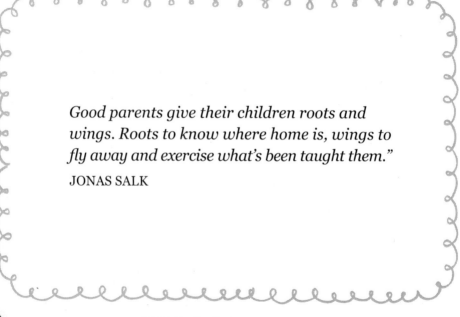

Good parents give their children roots and wings. Roots to know where home is, wings to fly away and exercise what's been taught them."

JONAS SALK

THE SIXTY SECOND FAMILY

Most people believe a future event will make them happy (when the children are older/ when I get a new job/when we move house), but really happy people don't think about their lives like that. Even though life may be far from perfect, they learn to appreciate the good bits. They grasp happiness – however small – now.

There are no perfect parents and there are no perfect children, but there are plenty of perfect moments along the way.

DAVE WILLIS

THE SIXTY SECOND FAMILY

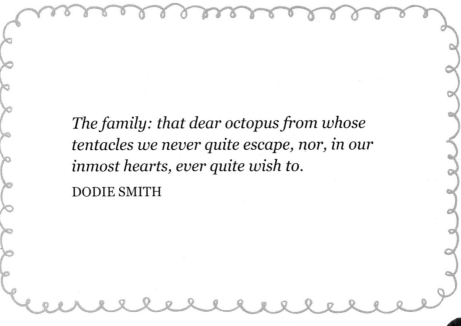

The family: that dear octopus from whose tentacles we never quite escape, nor, in our inmost hearts, ever quite wish to.

DODIE SMITH

Ultimately, if it works well, our family are those who will be there for us not because they think we're special, but because we are part of them. One thirteen-year-old girl put it like this:

"A family should trust each other and be nothing but themselves when around each

THE SIXTY SECOND FAMILY

other. A good family is not the perfect family like shown on TV, but the family that is happy overall and can help each other through bad times."

CHILDREN'S SOCIETY, 2009

Make that call to a sister, write a letter to that brother, don't lose heart with the teenager who's driving you crazy, reach out to that estranged child, don't take your husband or wife for granted – and if you have lost a love

THE SIXTY SECOND FAMILY

you once had for each other, perhaps try once more to rediscover it.

With all its joys, pains, fears and hopes ...

... this is your family.

About Care for the Family

Care for the Family is a registered charity and has been working to strengthen family life since 1988. Our aim is to promote strong family relationships and to help those who face family difficulties. Working throughout the UK and the Isle of Man, we provide parenting, relationship and bereavement support through our events, courses, training, volunteer networks and a great range of DVDs, books and online resources.

Our work is motivated by Christian compassion, and our resources and support are available to everyone, of any faith or none.

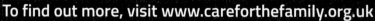

To find out more, visit www.careforthefamily.org.uk